BOOK REPORT POSTER PARTY

developed by Randy Marie Thorne
illustrated by Mella Cathleen

RANDY MARIE THORNE received a Bachelor of Arts degree in Elementary Education and Drama from New Mexico Highlands University. She is an experienced elementary teacher and has taught several in-service classes in New Mexico. Randy teaches fourth and fifth grades at the Taos Pueblo.

MELLA CATHLEEN attended Long Beach State University where she studied Interior Design and Art, and Fullerton College where she received an Associate of Arts degree in Graphic Technology. She is a free lance artist living in Southern California.

Copyright 1989 by THE MONKEY SISTERS, INC.
22971 Via Cruz
Laguna Niguel, CA 92677

ISBN 0-933606-73-7

BOOK REPORT POSTER PARTY

BOOK REPORT POSTER PARTY is a creative incentive program that provides a positive experience for the student. It provides an opportunity to encourage each student's reading endeavors while combining it with an exciting art poster to be colored and prominently displayed.

Each poster introduces the student to a different type of literature or book. The motivating format is intended to expand the student's interests in reading.

To use: Tear each poster at the perforation. If your school has a dry photocopier that accommodates 11x17 (28cm x 43cm), copy each poster directly onto this size paper.

If your school copier does not accommodate this size paper, we suggest carefully cutting the poster into two parts—along the fold line. Photocopy each part onto 8½x11 (21cm x 28cm). Students then carefully tape the two parts together (in the back) to give the effect of one large poster.

Encourage students to fill in the poster using their best handwriting. They may color the poster as a 'reward' after you have approved their written work on it. While thin-line markers make bright, appealing finished posters, colored pencil and/or crayon can also be used effectively.

Display finished work prominently for an appealing classroom environment. Plan a special display for parents' night and when visitors are expected. It will incorporate reading, language arts and art in a most pleasant manner.

CONTENTS

CHARACTERS

SETTING

SUMMARY

SCIENCE FICTION

TITLE

AUTHOR

TITLE _____

AUTHOR _____

SETTING _____

_____

_____

_____

MYSTERY

CHARACTERS

_____

_____

_____

_____

SUMMARY

_____

_____

_____

_____

_____

_____

MOST EXCITING PART

_____

_____

_____

_____

_____

_____

SCARIEST PART

_____

_____

_____

_____

BIOGRAPHY BANNER

PUBLISHER OF BOOK REPORT

DATE

_____
Title and Author of Book

DRAW A PICTURE OF THE MAIN CHARACTER DOING WHAT MADE HIM OR HER FAMOUS.

On _____
in _____
_____
was honored for _____
(describe a major event)
_____
_____
_____
_____
_____
_____
_____
_____
_____

Book Review

List two features (positive or negative) of this book that make it special for the reader.

_____
_____
_____
_____
_____

Interests and Hobbies

As a child, _____
(describe interests, hobbies and sports that the main character
enjoyed in his or her childhood.)
_____
_____
_____
_____
_____
_____
_____
_____
_____

DRAW A PICTURE OF A CHILDHOOD EVENT.

ANIMALS

BOOK FACTS

Title:

_____

Author:

_____

Setting:

_____

ANIMAL FACTS

_____ usually weigh

about _____ and are _____ in

height when full grown.

_____ like to eat

_____

There are _____ kinds or breeds of_____

Some of the different breeds are

_____

_____

The average lifetime of a _____ is _____ years

FUN FACTS

Draw a picture of 4 events or interesting facts that you remember from your book and write a short caption for each picture.

_____ _____ _____ _____

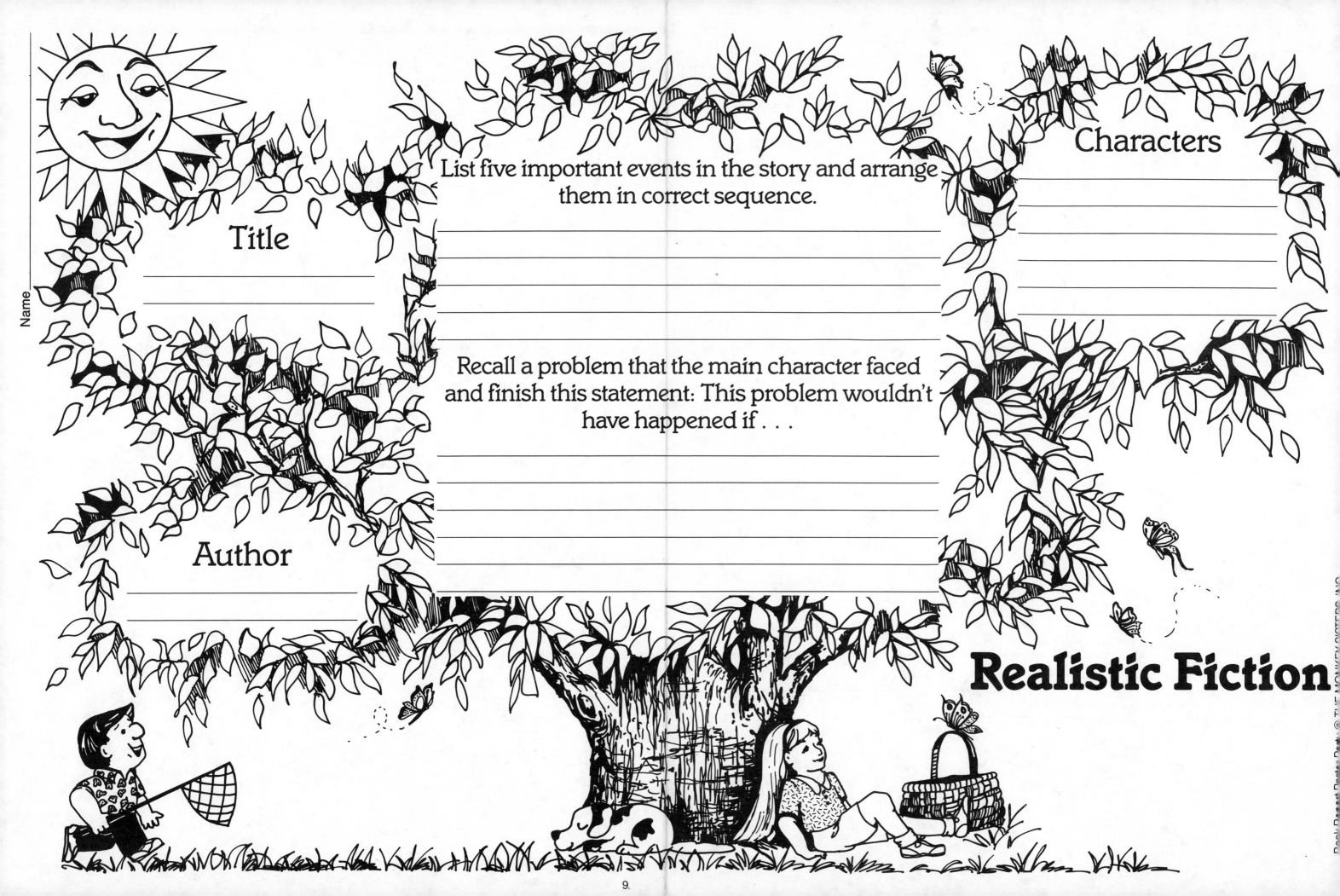

Name

Title

_____

_____

Author

_____

List five important events in the story and arrange them in correct sequence.

_____

_____

_____

_____

_____

Recall a problem that the main character faced and finish this statement: This problem wouldn't have happened if . . .

_____

_____

_____

_____

_____

Characters

_____

_____

_____

Realistic Fiction

9.

Title
_____
_____

Author
_____
_____

Characters
_____
_____
_____
_____
_____

Setting
_____
_____
_____

GROWING-UP

It often seems that you are either too old or too young to do certain things . . . .

Tell about one time the main character felt that he or she was too old to do something.

_____
_____
_____
_____
_____

Tell about one time the main character felt that he or she was too young to do something.

_____
_____
_____
_____

Tell about something that happened to make the main character happy to be the age he or she is.

_____
_____
_____
_____
_____

Name

Characters

Title

Author

Setting

ADVENTURE

I wish I could have been there when

I'm glad I didn't have to be there when

TITLE

AUTHOR

SETTING

FANTASY

SUMMARY

MOST
EXCITING PART

CHARACTERS

SPORTS

What qualities does a good player in this sport have?

List 7 Adjectives!

Title

Author

What would you need to achieve to be a "great" in this sport?

List 7 Verbs!

I chose to read about this sport because _____

Five new things I learned about this sport are:

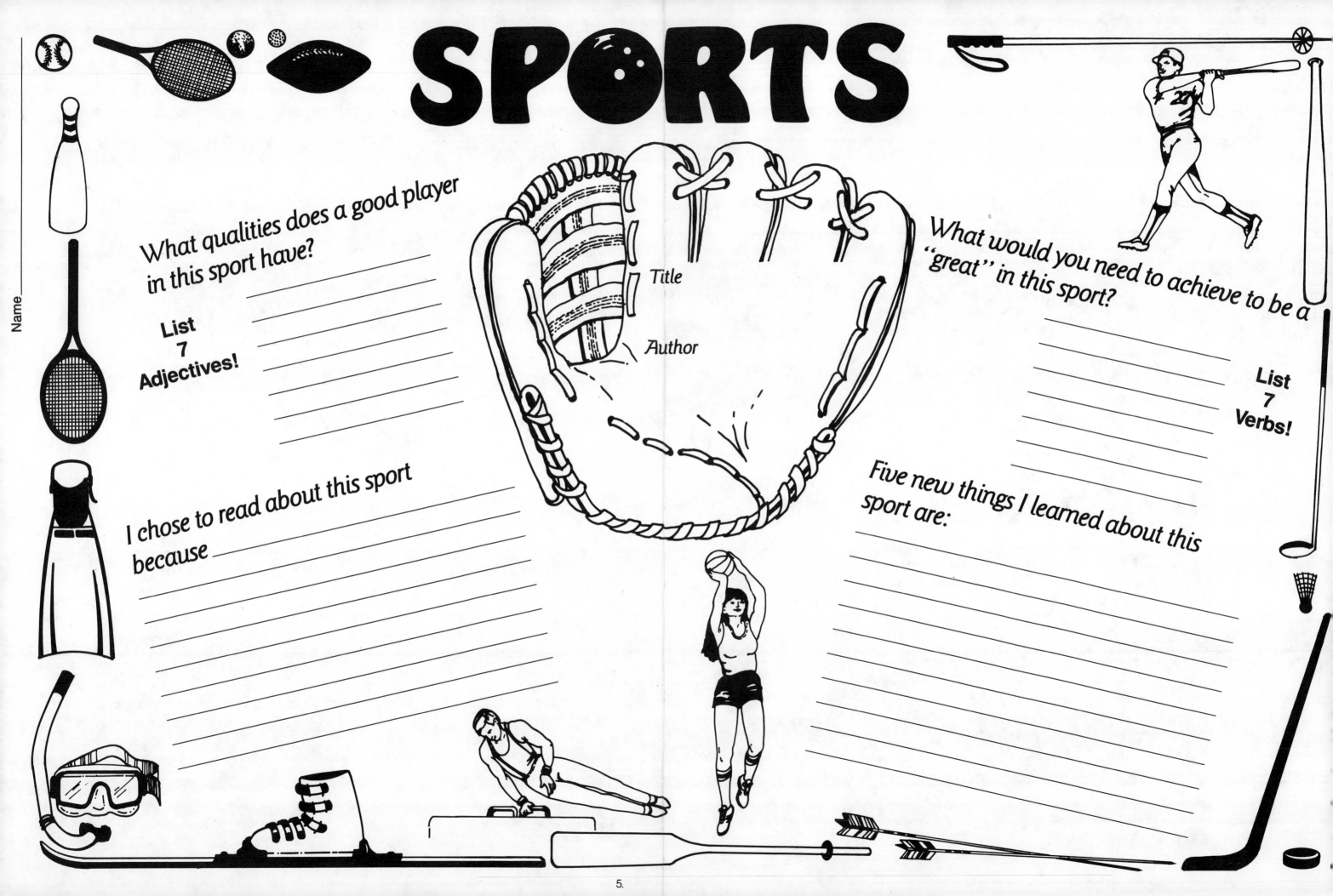

Folk Tales

Title *
_____

* Author
_____

Draw a picture of the setting of the story.

List the main characters and give two words to describe each one.

_____
_____
_____
_____
_____

Change the end of the story by changing a decision made by the main character. Discuss the new decision and its effects in the folk tale.

_____
_____
_____
_____
_____

Would the story (with the new ending) teach the same lesson it did with the original ending?
If so, what is the lesson?
If not, what is the new lesson?

_____
_____
_____
_____

HA! HA! HA! HA! HA!

Why would it be fun to have the main character as your best friend?

_____
_____
_____
_____
_____

Title
_____

Author
_____

Characters
_____
_____
_____
_____

Most humorous situations are funny only to the people not experiencing the situation. Describe one of these events from the book.

_____
_____
_____
_____
_____

What was the funniest part?

_____
_____
_____
_____
_____
_____

Describe a time in your life that everyone thought was funny— except you.

_____
_____
_____

HA! HA! HA! HA! HA!

Title

Author

List the steps you need to follow to complete this project.

1.

2.

3.

4.

5.

List the materials needed to complete a project described in this book.

Project: _____

Materials: _____

_____

_____

_____

_____

_____

HOW TO

What skills have you gained from doing this project that you can use in future projects?

_____

_____

What projects do you plan to try in the future?

_____

_____